NEW ANFIELD LEGEND
A Tribute To Robbie Fowler

To Pat

Best Wishes

NEW ANFIELD LEGEND

A TRIBUTE TO ROBBIE FOWLER

Bobby Blake

MAINSTREAM
PUBLISHING

EDINBURGH AND LONDON

Copyright © 1997, Bobby Blake

Photographs © Empics

First published in Great Britain in 1997 by
MAINSTREAM PUBLISHING COMPANY (EDINBURGH) LIMITED
7 Albany Street
Edinburgh EH1 3UG

ISBN 1 84018 010 2

A catalogue record for this book is available from the British Library

Designed by Ian McPherson

Printed and bound in Great Britain by The Bath Press Colourbooks, Glasgow

Contents

Goal Prowler Fowler

The game was barely 25 minutes old. Liverpool had been breaking forward in patches, but Arsenal, as always away from home, were defending manfully.

A Liverpool free-kick given 40 yards out from the Arsenal goal should have been meat-and-drink for what was widely regarded then as the best defence in the English league. But as it swung into the penalty area, legendary Liverpool Number 9 Ian Rush somehow got inside his marker, Martin Keown, and headed the ball down to where the 19-year-old lad they were calling 'the new Ian Rush' was waiting to meet it with his left foot, sending hapless Gunners goalkeeper David

Seaman the wrong way as he hit the ball first time into the net.

The roar from the Kop was still enveloping the ground as Steve McManaman picked the ball up inside his own half and began to glide towards the Arsenal goal. Perhaps anticipating the pass too eagerly, the Arsenal defence allowed him to dribble all the way to the edge of the area before finally moving in to intercept. But it was too late, as McManaman clipped the ball to his left where, once again, the pale-faced teenager in the red number 23 shirt was waiting to meet it, touching the ball just once to steady it before steering it with that magic left foot through defender Lee Dixon's legs and

Robbie Fowler's greatest domestic honour so far — lifting the Coca-Cola Cup at Wembley with Ian Rush

into the far corner of the Arsenal goal. Two goals; two minutes. And it wasn't over yet. Arsenal had charged at the left before sending the ball spinning into the space between Lee Dixon and Tony Adams where — you guessed

Two in two minutes — and it wasn't over yet!

Liverpool from the kick-off, determined not to let their heads drop despite the sudden double set back, clinging to the thought that if they could just pull one back before half time, they would still be in with a chance of levelling the match in the second half.

It was a notion they were swiftly disabused of, as John Barnes played a neat one-two for Liverpool to break down

it — that young Liverpool number 23 was already waiting to pounce. His defence beaten for pace, Seaman flew out of his goal to try and smother the shot, which he nearly managed to do, the ball bouncing as if in slow motion towards the safety of the touchline. But the best goalie in the world could only look on in despair as Liverpool's teenage terror ran on to lift the ball away from the line with his left foot before spooning it in with his right. Even the Kop, who had borne witness to the exploits of some of the greatest goalscorers in the history of the game, could hardly believe what they had just seen. Hat-tricks galore there had been down through the glory years at Anfield. But never one so quick or by one so young. And one of their own, too: a Liverpool scally from the top of his sometimes-blond head to the tips of his million-pound toes.

His name was Robbie Fowler and if the rest of the world didn't know it already they surely knew it now — not only was young Robbie going to be the new Ian Rush, the new Kenny Dalglish and the new Kevin Keegan all rolled into one, he was also going to be the biggest goalscoring talent Merseyside had ever produced.

It was August 28, 1994, and the four minutes it had taken him to put those three goals past the meanest defence in the country were enough to put the name Robbie Fowler into the record-books as scorer of the fastest hat-trick in Liverpool's 102-year history.

Afterwards, he was presented with the match-ball. "It's a great feeling to score three against the best defence in the country, let alone three in four minutes," Robbie told reporters as he clutched the ball to his chest. "It was great for us just to watch," quipped his delighted team-mate and close friend, Jamie Redknapp.

Robbie says now that it wasn't until he got off the pitch and someone pointed it out to him that he realised just how close the three goals were to each other.

"Scoring that hat-trick has probably been one of the best moments in my little career so far. To score three in that short space of time was brilliant for me, and for my family watching. They were all proud and jumping on their seats and that. Hopefully I'll do it again, but it'll take some doing next time, won't it?"

Indeed it will, but, as he's since proved, if anyone is capable of rewriting the record-books it's going to be Robbie Fowler.

He was just 21 when he hit the magical 100-goal mark in his 165th game for Liverpool (the 5–1 trouncing of Middlesbrough at Anfield, in December 1996, in which Robbie scored four of the goals). It was a quicker first

Robbie has begun to gain his England credentials

club in less time than it took Robbie — notching up his century in an astonishing 144 matches. But Hunt was in

He was just 21 when he hit the magic 100 mark

ton than even Ian Rush had notched up (he took 166 games). To put Robbie's achievement in even greater perspective, it's worth noting that it took Kevin Keegan 317 games for Liverpool to score 100 goals. And even Kenny Dalglish took 241 games to get his Liverpool ton.

Only Liverpool's World Cup-winning star of the Sixties, Roger Hunt, had scored his first 100 goals for the

his mid-twenties by then, and Robbie — injuries permitting — will almost certainly have scored his second century for the club by the time he reaches 25.

As a result, since that record-breaking hat-trick against Arsenal, Robbie has lost the 'new Ian Rush' tag and acquired an even more vainglorious nickname amongst his team-mates and fans. "We call him God," explains fellow

Larking around with Liverpool and England team-mate Mark Wright. Robbie is a relaxed guy off the pitch

Scouser Jason McAteer. "Because he does wondrous things!" Now valued in the £20 million-plus bracket, few unbiased observers would disagree with McAteer. When it

At 22, time is certainly on his side. The prolific brilliance of the England goal-getting partnership between Alan Shearer (age 26) and Teddy Sheringham (31) is unlikely to

"He's still only young — and always improving"

comes to the key areas for a centre-forward — skill, control, passing, heading, work-rate, temperament and pace — most coaches would probably mark Robbie somewhere in the eight to nine out of 10 bracket. His chief asset though is the most important quality a top-level striker needs — his finishing — and for this they would have to give him an unqualified 10 out of 10. The man is a modern-day, record-breaking marvel. And the most thrilling part of the Robbie Fowler story is that the best is yet to come.

As Steve McManaman says: "He's still only young but he's improving all the time. I don't see why he can't go on to break all the records before him."

survive past the next World Cup, in France. And with half-a-dozen England caps already to his name, plus the experience of having been a member of both Terry Venables's Euro 96 squad and — injuries allowing — Glenn Hoddle's World Cup 98 squad, Robbie will be perfectly poised to take his place in the side that will be battling for their place at Euro 2000.

Liverpool skipper and former England star John Barnes is just one professional pundit who thinks Robbie will lead the England side in the future.

"There are a lot of quality strikers but he has to be up there in the England manager's thoughts. If you are

Fowler demonstrates all of the qualities of the top striker — balance, power and an eye for goal

looking for goal-scorers, Robbie has to be up there with the best of them. He has the temperament, self-belief, arrogance, whatever you want to call it. And he won't be afraid of it when his chance comes."

Some might still see him as the bad boy of footie who is always photographed out at nightclubs, living it up with sexy models and actresses like Davinia Murphy (star of TV soap *Hollyoaks*) and hanging out with pop stars — or both, in the case of his and best mate Steve McManaman's appearance as guests of the Spice Girls at the 1997 Brit Awards. Indeed, some cynics have branded

Robbie, Stevie McManaman, Jamie Redknapp, David James and Jason McAteer as the Liverpool Spice Boys.

But that's unfair. As Jamie Redknapp is quick to point out when responding to those kind of accusations: "We care more about football at this club than anywhere else I know."

And nobody at Liverpool cares more about getting the ball in the back of the opposition's net than Robbie Fowler, the supreme finisher. "Every time that I go onto the pitch, I honestly believe I'm going to score," he says.

And these days so does everybody else.

Liverpool Lad

Robert Bernard Fowler was born in Kirby on April 9, 1975, and was brought up on a council estate in Toxteth, a poor working-class neighbourhood just a bus ride away from both Anfield and Goodison Park.

As a youngster he was actually an ardent Blues supporter who would turn up for PE lessons at school dressed in his full replica Everton strip.

"I was a proper Everton supporter when I was little," he admits. "I used to travel around to see them play with me dad and that."

These days, he cites Alan Shearer and Jurgen Klinsmann as his two favourite players, but boyhood heroes included Argentina's Diego Maradona and almost-as-good (honest!) Everton players like striker Graham Sharp and midfielder Trevor Steven.

Steve McManaman, another Liverpool scally who joined the club at 15, is three years older than Robbie and comes from the same sort of background. Like Robbie, he too was an Everton supporter as a schoolboy. (As was Ian Rush, strangely enough.)

He insists though that both he and Robbie are "Liverpool players and very proud of it. Although we were Everton fans as kids it still makes a big difference playing for a club in your home town. You have more of a relationship with the place, the supporters, everything about it."

As fellow-scally Jason McAteer points out, "It's not unusual to see both blue and red scarves hanging from the windows on a Merseyside derby day. We're all from the same city and we all have the same sense of humour and the same way of looking at things. We're all from Liverpool and we all just want to play football."

Robbie agrees. "Ever since I was little, I wanted to play football."

A regular goalscorer from the age of 11 for the Nugent Secondary School team, where he was a pupil, soon he was playing regularly for Liverpool Schools' Under-14 team where he was spotted by Liverpool scout Jim Aspinall, who immediately invited the astonished youngster to join the renowned Liverpool School of Excellence. He began training once a week with the rest of the youth sides at Melwood, the club's training ground, and signed schoolboy forms with the club when he was 14.

Another one for the mantelpiece

His abiding memory of that period in his life is scoring both goals for Liverpool Schoolboys in the 2—0 victory over Newcastle Schoolboys in the final of the Associated Schoolboy Cup, at Goodison Park of all places!

"It was the first time I'd actually played at a big ground," he recalls. "And with me being an Evertonian, it was a really special night."

Two years later, he left school and signed on as a 16-year-old YTS trainee. He would arrive at Melwood at nine o'clock every morning to begin his duties, which apart from training included getting all the players' kits laid out and ready for them, cleaning and restudding their boots, sweeping the corridors, even washing and scrubbing out the players' communal baths.

"And when you see the size of the baths you know that takes some doing," he smiles. "But everyone's got to start somewhere."

But once his tasks for the day were over, and Robbie started training, "That was brilliant!" he says. "Especially when you're training with the likes of Ian Rush, John Barnes and Peter Beardsley — players I looked up to."

Certainly, there can have been no better apprenticeship for the budding centre-forward than to have a genuine Liverpool goalscoring legend like Ian Rush there to learn first hand from. As Robbie now freely admits: "Probably everything I know, I've learned from Ian Rush. He has been a real father-figure to me and I couldn't have wished for a better teacher in my early days. He's been at the top for years and it's great for a young player like me to have the opportunity of playing alongside him."

Robbie was a regular goalscorer at school. It's a habit he's never managed to lose — or tried to!

But then, as Liverpool manager Roy Evans sagely points out: "Ian may be a good teacher, but Robbie's a good learner."

At 5ft 8ins in his socks and weighing just 11st 10lb, Robbie may not have had the classic centre-forward's brick out-house build, but he already knew how to knock the ball unerringly in the net with whatever part of his size-seven boots he was legally allowed to and he could head a ball better than most six-footers. Now he had to learn how to lose his marker, to find out how to feint and to know when to run, attributes that were already surfacing to stunning effect as he scored his way through both the 'B' and 'A' Youth teams in his first season as a 16-year-old trainee.

Even so, when Robbie turned professional and signed his first contract with Liverpool on his 17th birthday, in April 1992, he admits he was relieved to make the cut, as he watched several of his disappointed former school-team-mates either dropped outright or encouraged to find new clubs, usually lower down in the League.

"You get a lot of players who train and work really hard and they're told that they're not good enough. I was quite fortunate, 'cos I worked on my game and I wasn't a bad player so I was given a chance. A lot of it is natural talent, but you've still got to work on it anyway to improve. I can get better."

His dad, Bobby Fowler, was an enormous help, support-ing Robbie every step of the way — even giving up going to Everton games in order to watch his young son climb through the ranks at Liverpool.

"He's been to every game I've had since I was 11," reveals Robbie. "He's my biggest fan and he's my biggest critic as well. Never stops giving me stick."

"From ten upwards, really, people would say that he had a chance, if he went the right way," Bobby Fowler remembers. Not least the marvellous backroom staff at Anfield, who have been there from the word go to lend Robbie the kind of guidance and support you need to handle life at the top in the Premiership. Former star winger of the Liverpool title-winning side of the Seventies, now Director of Youth Football at Anfield, Steve Heighway, picked Robbie out early on as a potential superstar and offered him special encouragement and advice.

Thankfully, Robbie reacted to all the attention he was getting in all the right ways, and by the time he was 17 he had already outgrown the Youth teams and was now a reg-ular goalscorer in the full Reserve side.

"I was young, playing against men, and I enjoyed it," he recalls. Nerves were never a factor. "Once the first whistle goes, you just forget a lot of your nerves."

Jamie Redknapp, bought by Kenny Dalglish in 1991, first remembers noticing the 16-year-old Fowler banging in the goals at Melwood against seasoned first-team profes-sionals as though he'd been doing it all his life. "I remember him being like a right cheeky kid. I thought,

Robbie has moved from the streets of Toxteth to the company of stars — here with Pele and Les Ferdinand

Fowler quickly learned that every striker has to go in where it hurts

Feeling the force of Gareth
Southgate's boot against
Aston Villa

he's got so much ability and he's so sure of himself, he
can't really go wrong."

A lot of the most talented football trainees go to clubs in
cities miles from their family homes and end up living
together, much like students, in digs. This can be both pos-
itive in the sense of toughening young individuals up to
the realities of the outside world, but it can also mean they
take longer to adjust to their new lives. Living practically
on the doorstep of the club meant that Robbie was spared
all that. Indeed, even
though he now owns a
mansion in one of the
more posh Liverpool
suburbs, his mum still lives with him, while his dad, from
whom his mother is amicably separated, lives just around
the corner.

It all helped bond Robbie to not just the club but a whole
way of life. "Liverpool are a family club," says his father.
"And once you go and play for Liverpool I think you want
to be part of the club."

"He had so much ability..."

Liverpool, of course, is world-renowned for its footballing heritage — both as a city and as a club. It's been an
all-consuming passion that, over the years, has made
Anfield the home of some of the most remarkable and successful footballing sides and some of the biggest stars the
British game has ever known.

Manchester United will go down in history as the finest,
most successful English team of the Nineties, but not even
the most partisan of United fans would be able to
seriously compare
those successes to the
unprecedented trophy
hunting that the
magnificent Liverpool sides of the Sixties, Seventies and
Eighties indulged in. From the first League Championship
title legendary manager Bill Shankly steered the club to in
1964, to the current manager Roy Evans's reign and the
1995 Coca-Cola Cup victory, Liverpool won 13 League
Championships, five FA Cups, five League Cups (in its various guises as Milk, Rumbelows, Littlewoods and, latterly,

Scrapping hard for his
country against Croatia

Things moved fast when Robbie hit the big time

Coca-Cola), four European Cups, two UEFA Cups, and 13 Charity Shields.

But then no other club in the English games is ever likely to equal Liverpool's outstanding record of achievement. Most impressive of all though has been the club's unique footballing philosophy — a way of looking at not just football but at life that reflects the vibrant personality and tradition of the city that lends the club its name.

The words 'You'll Never Walk Alone' which adorn the wrought iron gates that open onto the ground are more than just the words to the Kop's most famous terrace-song — they are the message of Liverpool football club to the hundreds and thousands of supporters who walk through them. That the club and the city are one and the same.

Which is why it is even more fitting that the club's biggest star of the current side is himself just a local Liverpool lad with a head full of football and a dream of better things to come. Apt that in a time of spiralling transfer fees and grossly inflated wage claims, Robbie cost the club absolutely nothing.

As a harbinger of the future, Robbie could not have timed his entrance into the first team more perfectly. Liverpool, under then manager Graeme Souness, had won the FA Cup at the end of Robbie's first season as a trainee. But they ended the following season empty-handed and just sixth in the League, their joint-lowest position for 20 years. Now a disastrous start to the following 1993–4 season had left the club with four defeats in their last five matches as they set off for London to face Fulham in the first leg of the Second Round of that year's Coca-Cola Cup.

The first team had been plagued by injuries but there were still a great many surprised faces in the dressing room when Souness announced that their 18-year-old Reserve team striker would be making his debut at Craven Cottage that evening.

Roy Evans, who was working for Souness behind the scenes at the time, admits now that, "It started with Graeme Souness, to be fair. He threw Robbie in at that time when we weren't doing so well... Probably, if it had been me or Ronnie Moran, at the time, we'd have stayed with the more experienced ones. But sometimes you take a chance, as Graeme [did] with Robbie, and it [proves] very fruitful."

It was September 22, 1993 — an important date in the story of Robbie Fowler. The day he made his debut for the Liverpool first-team playing alongside his idol, Ian Rush, and, it almost goes without saying, scored the winning goal.

"It was all in the papers that there was gonna be a big change around, but when [Graeme] read the team out I was quite surprised," Robbie remembers. "But I got on the pitch and I really enjoyed it."

Robbie wore 23 and scored the third goal in a 3-1 win — a lovely slanting cross over the penalty area by then Liverpool wing-half Don Hutchison which Robbie hit first time on the half-volley, sending the ball rocketing into the roof of the Fulham net. Equally satisfying, from the manager's point of view, he had also had a hand in the first two goals. Though Robbie says now that his main memory of the game, apart from his goal, was "going down with cramp every two minutes near the end".

"Everyone is going to know his name now," said Graeme Souness in the tunnel afterwards. But, he insisted: "We'll do our best to make sure his life does not change one bit. I don't want to go overboard about him. But he is without doubt a very, very special talent who could go on to be the very best." Prophetic words indeed from the player who had won both League and European honours with the club in its early-Eighties prime.

In Robbie Fowler, Liverpool had found someone very special. They had found the future...

That trusty left
foot again...

A little local rivalry with
Jamie Redknapp in England
training

'The New Ian Rush'

If Graeme Souness had been "greatly encouraged" by Robbie's goal-getting debut in the first leg of Liverpool's Coca-Cola Cup tie against Fulham, his record-breaking performance in the return fixture at Anfield, on October 5, went beyond even the Kop's wildest imaginings.

That Liverpool should dust off the Division Two minnows 5–0 came as no real surprise to fans who had seen their club do worse to far more illustrious opponents more than once over the years. But that all five goals should be scored by the same scrawny teenager playing just his fourth match for the senior side was unheard of! Not since Ian Rush ten years before had a Liverpool play-

er scored five goals in one match — indeed, only four previous Liverpool players in the history of the club had ever managed the feat.

Three with the left, one with the right and one with the head. "That's gone down in history, that game," Robbie acknowledges with a smile. "Them sort of things, you only dream about. To score five goals at any level is an achievement and to score them in front of all the Liverpool fans — I was really made up."

Rush himself was quick to compliment the boy. "He always makes himself available — to tap a goal in here, tap a goal in there. He says I've helped him but at the end of the day, I think you've got to do it yourself. And

Robbie Fowler exploded into the Liverpool first team with a ferocity not seen since the arrival of Ian Rush

that's Robbie, you know, he wants to score goals. And when he scored five, you could see it in his eyes, he wanted to score six. And that's a true goalscorer for me, you know, no matter how many goals you've scored, you want to score more."

His first Premiership League goal was not long coming, either — grabbing the equaliser against Oldham, once again in front of the delighted Kop, on October 16. A long, hopeful header from Neil Ruddock into the Oldham box, where Robbie appeared to trap the ball with his right foot then hit it straight at goal with his left all in one fluid movement, was enough to give Liverpool a much-needed 2–1 victory.

"It hit me on the knee and then went through the goal-keeper's legs," Robbie confessed to the press after the match. "But they all count..."

Two weeks later, Robbie got his first League hat-trick in a blinding 4–2 victory against Southampton at Anfield that had the Kop believing — at least for a little while — that maybe the Liverpool of old were about to make a comeback.

Those feelings were perhaps premature, but under-standable after witnessing a stunning individual perfor-mance from their latest young prodigy, taking his tally to an unprecedented ten goals in his first eight games for the senior side. The first was a classic centre-for-

The infamous white suits on cup final day proved to be unlucky for Liverpool...

Graeme Souness may not have succeeded in everything at Liverpool, but he gave Fowler his opportunity

ward's goal — a long cross from right-back Rob Jones overlapping down the wing and a glancing header that sent the ball shooting through a huddle of defenders and into the net. The second was reminiscent of the young Ian Rush at his best, as Robbie skilfully chested down a pass on the edge of the box from McManaman, ran through and side-footed the ball with his right foot into the net. "That was a striker's goal," said John Barnes admiringly after the match.

His third goal that day was, in a way, the most spectacular of all: an angled shot from a free kick he took himself from the right of the Southampton penalty area. Rushy had dived in to try and rake the ball into the net but he missed it by inches and the ball went skidding straight into the net anyway! It was an extraordinary finale to a virtuoso solo performance and afterwards a beaming Graeme Souness brought Robbie with him to the post-match press conference, the youngster smiling bashfully for the cameras and microphones that surrounded him in earnest for what would merely be the first of many such encounters over the next few years.

Robbie did his best to appear cool about the whole thing, but it was plain to see the pleasure he rightfully took from his latest goalscoring feat. "Anyone would be pleased to score three in the Premiership, so I'd say it's better than the five I scored in the Coca-Cola Cup." From

The faith Graeme Souness showed
in Robbie put him on the road to
international football

He's only small, but Fowler can be a real handful for even the biggest defenders

Fowler of England. Many people believe Robbie will be the long-term replacement for Alan Shearer

now on, Robbie would become a fixture in the Liverpool first-team as the side struggled to mount a bid for the Premiership title. His next Premiership goal came at home to Aston Villa, on November 28, and was Robbie's most stunning yet — a superb back-headed flick from a Dominic Matteo corner straight into the opposite corner of the Villa goal. A magnificent strike that gave Liverpool the lead on the stroke of half-time and in a bitterly contested 2—1 victory.

Further headline-making strikes away to Sheffield Wednesday — a low shot through a packed penalty area to equalise and help lift Liverpool on to a 3—1 victory — and twice away to Tottenham — when he picked up the ball just outside the centre-circle, cleverly tapped it past Calderwood, then ran like a train at the goal before coolly sliding the ball past 'keeper Thorsvedt, and later

with a penalty, in a nail-biting 3—3 draw — meant that Robbie had now scored 13 goals in his first 12 games for the first-team. A better goals-per-game ratio than any Liverpool striker since Roger Hunt in the Sixties!

"I think he's just unbelievably lucky in the box and every one of them have just bounced off his knee and gone in all season, really," Steve McManaman joked at the time, but the name Robbie Fowler was now on the tips of every football pundit's tongue.

So much so, it came as no real surprise when, in November 1993, Robbie was called up to make his debut for the England Under-21 side against San Marino. He had already made a big impression on the England Youth team set-up when he helped the national Under-18 side to win the European Under-18 Championship the previous summer. But he had been an unknown then.

The goal machine closes in on Chelsea's Frank LeBoeuf in a Premiership clash at Anfield

Now with his record-breaking tally of goals making him the best-known new striker in the English Premiership, it felt like he had the whole footballing world watching him against San Marino, scrutinising his every move to see if the reports they had been reading in the papers and seeing repeated on television really told the truth when they said this kid could be 'the new Ian Rush'.

Robbie did not disappoint. In by now time-honoured Goal Prowler Fowler-style, he marked his debut with a

goal — a blistering left-foot strike in just the third minute. "He's a natural," Roy Evans said, shaking his head in admiration. "He's self-centred, he's greedy, and that's a good thing in a striker."

It seemed like every time Robbie played and at whatever level, he scored a goal. Who knows what heights he might have scaled with Liverpool in that fateful first season in the side if he had not fractured a fibula, forcing him to miss a crucial two-month period at the start of

The famous nose-band is actually needed: Robbie had suffered an adenoid problem until a recent operation

Another one bites
the dust...

Fowler in full flow: a sight Anfield has seen with delightful regularity over the past three seasons

1994 which coincided painfully with the end of the ill-starred Graeme Souness-era and the beginning of the current period of back-to-basics traditionalism under Roy Evans.

An embarrassing home defeat to lowly Bristol City in the Third Round of the FA Cup, in January 1994, had been the last straw for both Souness and the directors of the club and the beleaguered manager resigned without waiting to be asked straight after the match.

It was a sad end to the managerial dreams of a player who had captained Liverpool to the highest honours in the Eighties. Before he agreed to take over from Kenny Dalglish in 1991, Souness had been manager at Glasgow Rangers, whom he set on the path to last year's Celtic-equalling nine Scottish League Championships in a row by winning the first two for them as player-manager. At

the time he was appointed as the new boss at Anfield, he looked like the perfect choice — like King Kenny, Souness was a member of the great Bob Paisley's world-dominating side of the Seventies.

But Liverpool finished sixth at the end of Souness's first full season in charge (their lowest League position for 20 years), though he did lead them to their fifth FA Cup trophy that year. And in the signing of future England midfielder Jamie Redknapp and the introduction to the first team of such home-grown talents as Robbie Fowler and Steve McManaman, it could be argued that it was Graeme Souness who laid the creative foundations for the current Liverpool side.

But when Liverpool finished sixth again at the end of the 1992—3 season, and this time without the feel-good factor of winning another major trophy to cushion the

Jostling for position as Liverpool take on Europe...

disappointment, Souness knew the following season would be make or break for him. Robbie recalls Souness's departure from Anfield with regret. "He gave me my chance and I'll always be grateful for that," he says. "I liked [Graeme] and got on well with him. So I was a bit upset when he left. I'd broken my leg and hadn't been training, so I was away when he left and never got a chance to say goodbye to him."

Souness's replacement could not have been more different. Himself just another local Liverpool lad made good under the auspices of the old Shankly-Paisley regime, Roy Evans had led an undistinguished career as a player but had made his mark as one of the dependable 'boot-room boys' — as they used to call the back-room staff at Anfield in the days when Evans, Paisley, Joe Fagan and the rest of Shankly's staff used to congregate in the boot-room under the stand for a quiet drink after training and some straight talking about the subject closest to all their hearts: Liverpool FC. Each one of them had eventually become manager and now, it seemed, it

was the turn of the man with the quiet smile and the nerves of steel who had seen it all in a career at Anfield that spanned three decades. Evans was one of the faithful. He would bring back The Liverpool Way that so many close to the club had felt Souness had misguidedly deserted with his expensive signings and intimidating dressing-room presence.

Fortunately for Robbie, with Evans already an ever-present in the first-team set-up, the adjustment at the club would not mean he would have to prove himself all over again to a completely new manager. All he had to do was concentrate on recovering his fitness and Roy would surely give him back his chance in the side. Which is exactly what happened.

Evans had been in charge of the side for two months when he decided to throw the newly-fit Robbie into his first Merseyside derby as Liverpool took on Everton at Anfield, on March 13, 1994. Determined to pick up with the side under Evans exactly where he had left it with Souness, Robbie managed to do just that as he scored

Robbie hurdles a tough
challenge from Paul
McGrath, then of Derby

A rare one with
the right boot!

The feeling no striker can describe: Fowler turns away to celebrate as one hits the back of the net...

the winner — a slide-rule pass from Barnes down the left for Robbie to pounce on — in a topsy-turvy 2–1 victory that could have gone either way were it not for Robbie's timely intervention.

"It's like a schoolboy's dream when them kind of things happen, and it's happened to me," Robbie told the Sky TV cameras afterwards, still hardly able to believe it himself. "It was at the Kop end as well which made it even more special," he says now. "Neville

[Southall] was one of my heroes when I was growing up, so to score past him was brilliant!" Ironically, it was that other former Everton supporter, Ian Rush, who got the other goal. Suitably impressed, Evans decided there and then to keep the Rush-Fowler striking partnership together.

Not only would the experienced Rush be able to pass on goalscoring tips to his goal-hungry understudy, he would be a useful ally in helping keep the 18-year-old's feet

Robbie finished his first full season in the Liverpool side as top scorer, with 18 goals in 33 matches

firmly placed on the ground. "On the staff side, we've tried to make him realise that it's about team performances and not just individual performances, although they obviously become a big part of Robbie's game with the goals he scores," Evans explained.

Although he was eventually unable to sustain his phenomenal goal-per-game ratio throughout the rest of the season as Liverpool struggled to finish eighth (their joint-lowest position since re-joining the top flight in 1962), and despite being out with injury for eight weeks, remarkably Robbie still finished his first season in the senior Liverpool side as their leading goalscorer with 18 goals from 33 matches in all competitions. He had made

28 League appearances, either in the starting line-up or brought on as sub, from which he had scored 12 of his goals; just two less than Rush had managed during that entire year.

"People don't recognise you at first, but they're all recognising Robbie now," observed Rush. "There's true potential there [but] next season's a big test for him." One that Rushy felt sure the youngster would pass with the flying colours of every team he scalped with his goal power. "Everyone at the club here, they don't really worry because they know he can come through."

Jamie Redknapp agreed with the expert summary of Ian Rush. "The way he's going I think he's just going to get more. Robbie's just a natural born striker..."

Providing chances for others
is also a growing part of the
Fowler repertoire

Natural Born Striker

As Ian Rush says, the real test for any young striker trying to establish himself in the Liverpool first team isn't just how well they do in their first season for the club, but how well they manage to perform during their second.

Second time around opposition defenders would be watching out for him, and the cameras would be there not just to praise but to criticise and judge. How well Robbie stood up to those pressures would be key factors in determining his future at the club.

Fortunately for the Fowler household, Robbie proved himself to be an exceptionally gifted student. Starting with a brilliantly taken opportunist's goal away to Crystal Palace, sparking a searing 6—1 demolition on the opening day of the 1994—5 season, Robbie would nearly double his goal tally of the previous season, making him the first Liverpool striker to score more than 30 goals in a season since Ian Rush seven years before.

It would take an entire book to go into the details of every single goal, but needless to say there were certain highlights that must rate a mention.

Robbie followed his opening day salvo against Crystal Palace with the record-breaking four-minute hat-trick against Arsenal at Anfield on August 28, and continued scoring right up until Christmas when he bagged the winning penalty in a tense 2—1 victory away to Leicester on

Fowler holds off former team-mate David Burrows, now of Coventry

Robbie turns up as a town crier, along with John Barnes and Ian Rush at the Liverpool Christmas party

Boxing Day. As Steve McManaman commented afterwards: "Robbie Fowler can't stop scoring at the minute. And I hope it continues that way." "We always thought it would get harder for him as time went on, but it looks as if it's getting easier," said Barnesy.

The 'new Ian Rush' tag had stuck but the goal-poacher Robbie most resembled in the minds of most long-time observers was that of former Tottenham and England striker Jimmy Greaves — the same stooped figure and unexpected bursts of speed, the same almost cheeky way they grabbed their goals, delighted whether they were inch-perfect shots from 30 yards or simple tap-ins amidst a scramble of bodies.

Greavesy, now a well-known TV pundit, certainly rated the young contender. "If he can bang them for England like he does for Liverpool, I think the sky's the limit for him," he predicted.

"A lot of it is down to confidence," says Robbie with a shrug. "If you're playing well and scoring goals, then you feel as though every time you go onto the pitch you can score... if you're having a bad time and not scoring goals,

it can work against you. But at the minute, every time I go onto the pitch I honestly believe that I'm going to score."

Few goals can have been more important to Liverpool's season that year than the last-gasp winner Robbie scored against Crystal Palace in the first leg of the Coca-Cola Cup semi-final, at Anfield, on February 15. Two minutes into injury time, McManaman made one last burst down the right flank, hitting a hopeful cross-field pass into the Palace penalty area which Rushy was just denied the space to slide home. But the ball fell free to Robbie on his right foot and suddenly, much to the delight of the relieved Kop, Liverpool were going into the second leg 1-0 up.

The cream on the cake, though, came in that fateful return at Selhurst Park on March 8, as Robbie scored with a run that began in the centre circle and finished in the Palace penalty box with a swerving left-foot grass-cutter. Robbie's 27th goal of the season had fired Liverpool into their first Coca-Cola Cup final for 11 years, and their first major final under Roy Evans.

Evans could not have been more pleased. Especially as in between the two Palace games Robbie had also scored

Fowler picked up his first honours in 1995, when Liverpool won the Coca-Cola Cup

his first ever FA Cup goal for Liverpool, in the desperately close 1—1 draw at home to Wimbledon in the Fourth Round on February 19.

"He's been a revelation, to be fair," said Evans. "To score 30-odd goals in your first full season..." he shook his head and smiled, unable to put into words the scale of the achievement. "And he's played in every game, which again is únbelievable really, at the age of 19."

"A lot of people have said that the second season is the hardest, but I've enjoyed every minute of it," said Robbie. "If anything, the goals seemed to be coming even easier."

"He's got this knack," said Stevie Mac as he considered his friends talents. "I mean, sometimes he'll go and miss a sitter, then five minutes later he'll score a 20-yarder. And I mean, he's only 19, so what can you say about him?"

The fickle finger of fate would determine that, having scored the goals that got Liverpool to Wembley that year, Robbie himself would not score in the final. Instead, it was the player who had become his best mate in the first team, Steve McManaman, who bagged both strikes in a pulsing 2—1 victory against First Division fighters Bolton — his first ever taste of a Wembley final though, and Liverpool's first trophy under new manager Roy Evans, it was a day that Robbie says he will never forget, whatever glories the future may hold.

"Ever since I was little, it's really been a big dream of mine to play at Wembley. To win my first medal there with Liverpool was really unbelievable. Walking out to the crowd and that — the crowd was brilliant. I just really want that more and more."

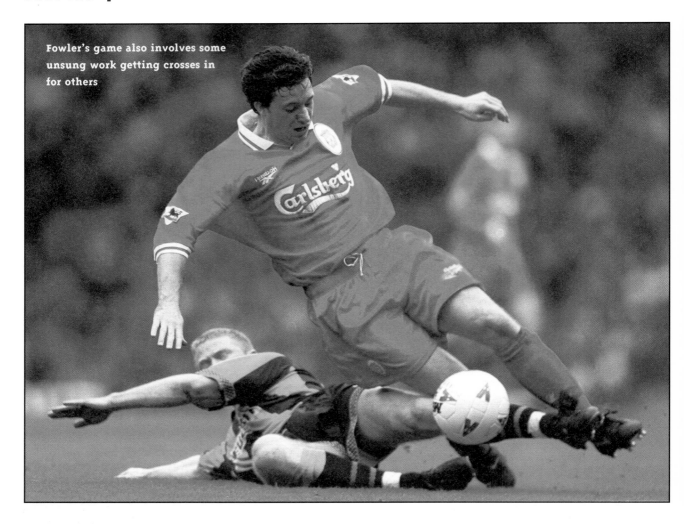

Fowler's game also involves some unsung work getting crosses in for others

At the end of the match, after the players had all received their medals and paraded the Cup in a lap of honour around the ground, Robbie went over to where his dad was seated in the crowd to show him his medal. Bobby could hardly believe his eyes. It was hard to tell who was more delighted, father or son.

Robbie let his dad take the medal away with him — a kindly gesture he nearly lived to regret when Bobby accidentally dropped the medal as he approached the car park and it almost rolled into a drain! Luckily though he retrieved it before it disappeared down the grate. Which is just as well. "I'd have strangled him," Robbie chuckles.

It wasn't the only glittering memento Robbie picked from his first full season in the side. In March, he was voted the Professional Footballers Association (PFA) Young Player of the Year. Almost at once, the clamour began for his inclusion in the full England squad.

To be honoured in such a fashion by his fellow professionals was heady stuff. "I'm gobsmacked!" But to be spoken of as a future England star was something else. "The idea of me being talked about as a possible England squad member is something I couldn't have dreamed of," he told reporters at the ceremony in London.

Liverpool chased Manchester United and the eventual winners Blackburn all the way to the end of the Premiership, but could only finish fourth that season. Still, with the Coca-Cola Cup back in the trophy cabinet at Anfield, both Roy Evans and Robbie Fowler had reason to be pleased with their progress in 1994–5.

Remarkably, Robbie had played in all 57 of Liverpool's games that season and was comfortably the club's leading scorer with 31 goals — including 25 goals from all 42 League matches (only Alan Shearer scored more League goals that year), plus two in the FA Cup and four in the Coca-Cola Cup.

The following season found the Liverpool side in transition. Bolstered by success in the Coca-Cola Cup and the return to European competition it brought them, Roy Evans was looking to fashion a new Liverpool side for the Nineties; one that was good enough to win the Premiership title — the only title that ever really matters up at Anfield.

David James had now permanently replaced Bruce Grobbelaar in goal and more new faces were being bought in, like the £3.5 million-pound signing, Jason McAteer. Evans's most significant signing that season

Performing somersaults as Liverpool attempt to reassert the dominance of Europe they had in the Seventies

Magic moment: Fowler heads his first-ever international goal against Mexico in the 2–0 win at Wembley

though would have a lasting effect on Robbie's role in the new side: that of Stan Collymore, an £8.5 million summer arrival from Nottingham Forest.

With Ian Rush still commanding the Number 9 shirt, that meant three forwards chasing just two places and the pressure was back on Robbie to perform and stay in the side. Adding to the burden, Roy Evans chose to start the season with Collymore partnering Rush up front and Robbie on the bench. The manager had been quoted in

was Robbie's 50th goal for Liverpool in two years and suddenly it was Stan who was chasing his place in the side.

Once again, it's impossible to list the details of every single one of the 36 blinding goals Robbie scored that season, but certain highlights will always stand out. Not least Liverpool's home game against Bolton on September 23. It was Robbie's 100th game for the first-team, and of course he had to mark the occasion with something special — a fantastic four goal feast (all four with that sweet

"I needed a kick up the backside."

the national press as saying that "Robbie Fowler's attitude wasn't right".

Robbie, who had recently dyed his dark locks blond, took it all in his stride and even later agreed with the Liverpool manager. "I needed a kick up the backside because in hindsight I was taking my place in the first team for granted. The manager just showed me that I wasn't right in that."

However, Collymore's absence through injury for Liverpool's third game of the season away to Tottenham, on August 26, handed Robbie his first start of the season. "If I play I'll be delighted but disappointed because Stan's injury is giving me the chance," he said. "But if I get my chance I'll make the most of it." A promise he duly kept, banging in the third and winning goal from a Stevie Mac cross from the right wing in a brilliant 3–1 victory. It

left foot) in a magnificent 5–2 trouncing of their fellow North-Westeners!

"I was just pleased to get one," he shrugged modestly afterwards. "And then the second came, and then the third, and then the fourth…" he shook his head. "After the fourth one, I just wanted more…"

And of course there was Robbie's scene-stealing performance the following week at Old Trafford, in the game that would see the return of Eric Cantona to the Manchester United starting line-up after his nine-month suspension for the kung-fu attack on a supporter during a match against Crystal Palace at Selhurst Park the previous season.

Robbie was determined to upstage the Frenchman, scoring two headline-grabbing goals in a thrilling 2–2 draw. Robbie, though, was quick to point out that, "It's a

Robbie listens up during
England training

All-action hero: Fowler stretches hard and low to find the fateful finishing touch...

team game and if the team's playing well, we'll be getting chances. And luckily enough, I've been on the end of most of them."

On their day the new Liverpool were better, according to many impartial observers, than even United — as Alex Ferguson's men found out to their cost in the return at

Robbie, as he managed to score in every round of the competition. "I wanna win the FA Cup and then go round Liverpool on a bus," he said. "It's just something I've wanted to do since I was little. I've seen teams come home with the FA Cup and go round the city and that's really all I've wanted to do."

"I was just pleased to get one. But after the fourth goal I still wanted more"

Anfield when Robbie ran riot and scored both the goals again in an unforgettable 2—0 victory that sent the Kop into raptures. Robbie's own personal bit of double-trouble for the double-double winners to contend with!

After an indifferent start, Robbie's partnership with Collymore would result in 54 goals between them that season. But still it was only good enough to take Liverpool to third in the League. "Liverpool had a great team that year," Collymore remembers. "How we never won nothin', I don't know…"

Perhaps the bitterest pill they were forced to swallow that year though was losing to their deadliest rivals, Manchester United, in the final of the FA Cup. Up till the final, the Cup had been another personal triumph for

As with the Coca-Cola Cup the previous year, Robbie had been the star of the semi-finals, scoring two of the goals in Liverpool's commanding 3—0 victory over Aston Villa at old Trafford, on March 31.

But his hopes were to be dashed in that strangely lacklustre FA Cup final performance. It's true that Liverpool had the better of the play on the day, but once again it was United and their mercurial Frenchman who scored the only goal and walked off with the silverware.

With years still ahead of him, Robbie could afford to be philosophical, though. "There's always next year," he said, and he was right.

Once again, Robbie ended the year on a personal high when he was voted the PFA's Young Player of the Year for

Sharing a joke with reporters at an England press call

the second year running. Speaking at the ceremony, Jamie Redknapp said: "Robbie's got everything for me. He's a fantastic goalscorer at such a young age, he just bangs in goals for fun. I've never seen anyone so good at his age. And I'm just so pleased he plays for Liverpool."

And once again the call came for his inclusion in the full England side. This time, however, the Fowler-fans in the media got their wish when the England coach brought Robbie on as a sub for Ian Wright, late in a friendly at Wembley against Bulgaria the same month.

"Once you play for England, you want to play again, so it just whets your appetite really," Robbie said afterwards. "So I'd love to play again and hopefully get a few more chances in an England shirt."

over title-chasing Newcastle United, at Anfield on April 3. As Robbie says: "It was always going to be a big game but no-one expected it to be the score line that it turned out to be."

The memory of that topsy-turvy classic still makes Stan Collymore's head shake with awe. "It'll go down as a classic," he says. "I mean, I've never played in a game like it and I'm sure Robbie hasn't."

Stan it was who provided the deep cross from the left in the second minute that Robbie met with a perfectly angled downward header which bounced once before plunging into the net. "It went in off me nose," he later explained, but like he said, they all count: 1–0. Then Newcastle scored two quick goals to lead 2–1 at half-time.

Steve McManaman looks on as Robbie slips the ball home. This one, though, was ruled offside...

He wouldn't have to wait long, Venables granting the youngster his first full cap when he included him in the England starting line-up for the first time for their Euro 96 warm-up against Croatia, in April. With McManaman there to assist, Robbie put an early opportunity over the crossbar and never quite recovered. But the coach kept him on for 90 minutes and would eventually find a place for Robbie in the squad he would assemble for the Euro 96 finals that summer.

As Collymore says: "Robbie can make the central striking position [for England] his own in the next ten years. It's down to him."

But his most incredible performance of the season was surely the amazing 4–3 victory Robbie helped Liverpool to

Then, nine minutes into the second half, McManaman snaked into the box and hit a hard square pass to Robbie who hit it first time into you know where; 2–2.

When Newcastle got back to 3–2, the Kop were in despair. Surely there could be no way back. Then Stan scored two unbelievable goals to make it 4–3 and Kevin Keegan was left facing the fact that his managerial dreams had been crushed on the very pitch where his own Championship career as a player had begun 20 years before. Today, Geordies everywhere will tell you, "That was the match that lost us the Championship."

Ironically, if Liverpool had not won that night, then Manchester United might not have gone on to win the League. But then, football's a funny old game, as some-

Fowler reaches out that golden left leg to pull the ball down in another close encounter in the box

one somewhere else is probably saying right now. Once again, Robbie ended the season as Liverpool's top scorer; his final tally was 36 goals in all competitions, including 28 goals from all 38 League games. And again, only Alan Shearer had scored more goals in the Premiership. But even he was starting to look over his shoulder. Robbie Fowler's wonderful natural talent was beginning to be hardened by a professional's cold eye for the kill.

49

Spice Boy?

These days it seems the name Robbie Fowler gets almost as many mentions in the gossip columns as it does in the sports pages. And though he insists he's still more of a mummy's boy than a toy boy, he's certainly had his share of 'scrapes' since becoming famous.

He admits he's no saint, but then what normal, healthy, fit and curious 22-year-old lad is? "The 'scally' thing has been over-exaggerated," Robbie says simply. "I've never been a bad lad. It's just that everything you do gets scrutinised. But I've been getting picked on because I've done one or two silly things, and people think I'm going to carry on like that all the time, which I'm not."

Robbie's bad boy image can be traced back to a Boxing Day match against Leicester City in 1994, when he decided to hitch up his shorts in front of the Filbert Street crowd after scoring the winner in a gesture that could not generally be interpreted as friendly (ahem!) — an incident Roy Evans put down to "youthful exuberance" from a lad who was not yet 20 but which would later result in a £1,000 fine from the FA for 'bringing the game into disrepute'.

Just a few weeks previously though, Robbie had been sent off for the first time in his senior career during an England Under-21 international in Austria, for which he was suspended by UEFA for four games. Then there was the

Robbie holds off Newcastle's Philippe Albert in the 'Match of the Decade' Part One at Anfield

incident the following season when Roy Evans was reported to have fined Robbie a hefty sum for being caught breaking the club's strict curfew laws, dancing the night away at a Liverpool club on the eve of an important game.

And of course there were the infamous photographs and reports of Robbie and the England party 'living it up' on their pre-Euro 96 tour of the Far East. The pictures of various members of the England squad taking turns in the 'dentist's chair' at Hong Kong's most notorious night-spot,

the Jump Club, were splashed across the front pages of the tabloids — shots of players with their shirts ripped open and bottles of tequila being poured down their throats. Funny at the time no doubt, but hardly the most auspicious image to present to the folks back home on the eve of hosting the European Championships.

Steve McManaman, who was also present that night, attempts to put the whole thing into perspective: "We were out for Gazza's birthday, the players hadn't had a drink all

Robbie takes the aerial route after a challenge with Chelsea's England winger Dennis Wise

tour, it was two weeks before the start of the [European] Championships and the people in the bar said we were absolutely no trouble."

"His ability is undoubted," says Roy Evans. "We've just got to make sure that he keeps his feet on the floor. Not only us, his dad's got to kick him up the backside. That's important when you're getting high media publicity week in, week out — that somebody makes sure you don't get beyond your means."

Fortunately, Robbie comes from a very down-to-earth family. His sternest critic is still his dad, Bobby, who says he is convinced his son will "do the right thing. He's not a big head, by any means."

"I wouldn't say he's quiet," smiles Jamie Redknapp. "He's one of the lads and he's always the first to go out and have a good time. [But] he's just a really nice lad, which is the most important thing."

Robbie has never had a problem taking the time to sign autographs and talk to people. "Liverpool fans are the best in the world," he says proudly. "It's the same faces every week, it's like a family." But the glare of the media can be

intrusive, too, and he admits that he has found it hard to come to terms with the constant attention. "I thought you just played football," he says. "I never expected the downside of the press trying to stitch you up and that."

Like Jamie Redknapp and Steve McManaman, Robbie is now tied to a lengthy and lucrative deal with the club. But his earnings are boosted by the various sponsorship, advertising and promotional opportunities that have been thrust his way since he became Liverpool's top scorer.

Robbie has never been one to discuss figures — "I don't think about the money" — but it's not hard to imagine the kind of sums he can now command for his services. It's the same throughout the team.

All the lads have done modelling assignments. David James appeared on 50-foot-high posters in Armani underpants; Jamie Redknapp regularly advertises a well-known skin cream. And though the Liverpool team is sponsored by Reebok, Robbie has also appeared in TV ads for sports manufacturers Nike.

As a result, critics have dubbed the Anfield dressing room Football's Catwalk, and Robbie, Jason, Jamie,

Robbie's had a few scrapes off the pitch, as well as on — in this case with the German side Brann Bergen

Stevie Mac and David James have become known as Liverpool's Spice Boys.

"Okay, a few of our lads have got modelling contracts. But when it comes down to the nitty-gritty on the football pitch the so-called model boys will be first there in the thick of the action," notes Robbie.

Jamie Redknapp is even more emphatic: "It gets on my nerves all the crap that's levelled at us — that we were more interested in modelling than winning medals. We care more about football at this club than anywhere else I know.

"There are guys back here for extra training morning and afternoon. But we know we will get things thrown at us until we win something again."

Robbie's best mate in the team is Steve McManaman, with whom he claims to have a special understanding. "We have a laugh and on the pitch it just naturally takes off," says Steve. On away trips, they room together. On non-match days, training at Melwood is usually followed by lunch with Stevie Mac and the rest of the lads at either Est est est or The Armadillo, both happening local drink-and-eateries in Liverpool's fashionable Albert Docks area.

Although he has never met his favourite actress Demi Moore, he has escorted more than one famous lovely in his time, including Emma 'Baby Spice' Bunton (after Robbie and Stevie Mac were guests of the Spice Girls at the Brits awards ceremony last year) and the sultry Davinia Murphy, star of TV soap *Hollyoaks*.

In close contact with
Holland's Aaron Winter

Robbie still takes stick from the lads for an early interview — but he's learned his lesson now...

Recently, the papers have pictured Robbie on nights out with Andrea Boardman, daughter of comic Stan Boardman.

An interview with *Loaded* magazine fanned the flames of infamy. "I still get stick off the lads for that one," Robbie sighs ruefully. "When you first get interviewed, you're naive and that, and you're not really sure what to say. I've never really changed as a person, but I've learnt. I'm not really stupid in what I say now. I'm quite sensible. I'm not a bad lad anyway, full stop."

To prove it, he recently moved himself and his family from the council estate in Toxteth to a mock Tudor mansion in one of the more posh Liverpool suburbs. His mum still lives with him at the house, cooking and cleaning for him. "Me mum's a great cook — that's my excuse, anyway. But I'd be lost without her. I can't do nuthin' without her." And although he's taken to enjoying a round or two of golf every week with the lads from the team (his handicap is 18),

he still spends most of his spare time hanging out with the same gang of mates he grew up with on the streets of Toxteth.

For 'vibes', he digs into his huge collection of soul music classics (vinyl and CD). Robbie enjoys watching TV, too, but don't ask him to sit down and watch a match on the TV with you. "I hate watching live games," he says, "no matter who's playing, in case they're o—o and boring. You've sat down for an hour and a half and not seen nothing."

Clearly, Robbie is one of life's do-ers; he's not a watcher. These days, he says, all he really, really wants is to bring that elusive League title back to Anfield where he says it belongs.

"I am quite a sensible lad and I hope people will look at me in a different way now. If you want to succeed at this level you've got to keep your feet on the ground and that's what my family and friends help me do."

The New Number Nine

Robbie Fowler was nine when Ian Rush won his first Golden Boot award for the most League goals in a season. If anyone had told the young Everton supporter back then that one day it would be he who replaced Rushy in that red Liverpool number 9 shirt, no doubt they would have been greeted with a mixture of scorn and disbelief. But that's exactly what happened at the start of the 1996–7 season.

Now in his mid-thirties, Rushy was encouraged to make a move to Leeds United before retiring. It was the end of one era and the beginning of another — the passing down of the red number 9 made easier by the knowledge that it was going to a good Scouse home. "Robbie can go on to

smash my record of 335 goals in 645 games for Liverpool," said Rushy generously. "With his talent, I would also back him to beat Roger Hunt's 245 League goals for the club."

Robbie certainly set about the new season with renewed enthusiasm, scoring two blistering goals in Liverpool's opening-day 3–3 bonanza away to Middlesbrough. But a nasty back injury — the first of many that would bedevil him throughout the season — meant that Robbie was forced to sit out England's first World Cup qualifying match against Moldova, on September 1.

Coming on as a sub twice (against Holland and Spain) during England's semi-successful Euro 96 campaign had given Robbie a head start when it came to inclusion in new

A valuable lesson from coach Venables: The England coach acknowledged Fowler's international potential

England manager Glenn Hoddle's first squad. But although he travelled down to meet Hoddle, it was clear that he had no chance of making the flight to Kishinev. "The more important thing for me was to get him down here and have a chat," Hoddle explained. "To go another five weeks without that chance would have been foolish."

Robbie had recovered in time for Liverpool's first match of the European Cup Winners' Cup, away to MyPa 47 Anjalonkoski of Finland, on September 12. In the only European competition the Reds have never won, they kicked off with a solid 1—0 victory, courtesy of a rare goal from Stig Inge Bjornebye.

Robbie was out again, however, for another three weeks with an ankle injury picked up at Melwood before the second leg against MyPa 47. Liverpool won comfortably again but life on the treatment table was beginning to get Robbie down. He had again been called up for the England squad that was to play Poland in the World Cup qualifier at Wembley in October, but once again was forced to miss out.

Robbie's absence was beginning to affect Liverpool, too. Many fans felt that they were only missing Robbie to beat Manchester United at Old Trafford, on October 12, where they'd had the better of the game but simply couldn't score. A goal from United's David Beckham meant Liverpool slipped to their first defeat of the season, and it cost them the leadership of the Premiership.

When he did come back, in a match away to FC Sion in the Second Round of the Cup Winners' Cup, he did his best to make-up for lost time, thumping home the equaliser in a close-fought 2—1 victory. It was Robbie's first European goal. Determined that it would not be his last, he scored another brace of stunners in the return fixture at Anfield on October 31, as Liverpool romped home 6—3 in a tremendous match that recalled the team's glory years in Europe.

Glenn Hoddle continued to show faith in Robbie and called him up for the England squad again for the World Cup qualifier against Georgia, on November 9. With Alan Shearer out with a groin injury, Robbie arrived in Tbilisi hoping Hoddle would give him a try. In the event, the England manager decided not to gamble on a striker not yet 100 per cent fit, but the experience put Robbie one step closer to fulfilling his dream.

"I'm still not at my sharpest," Robbie admitted. "But I'm sharp enough to do a job for England and I'm still hopeful the boss will give me the opportunity. I would give anything to get my first goal for England."

Meanwhile, back home he was surprised to discover he was just two goals short of scoring 100 for Liverpool. "I thought I'd scored about 80," he said. His big moment finally came against Middlesbrough, at Anfield on December 14. Scoring four goals in a stunning 5—1 victory, Robbie kicked off an extraordinary match with an unbelievable goal — scored in just 27 seconds! Collymore had

Liverpool fans are convinced that Fowler can spearhead a genuine title challenge next season...

run from just outside his own penalty area to the edge of the Middlesbrough area, where he stroked the ball with pin-point accuracy to Robbie who hit it first time past the hapless Walsh. As Steve McManaman ran over to congratulate him, Robbie pretended to look at his watch and shook his head. So did everybody else in the ground.

His second goal — and 100th for Liverpool — was a typical poacher's goal, catching Collymore's rebound off the post. Two more magnificent solo efforts gave him the first two goals of his next 100, but he had marked his 100th goal by running over to the touchline and pulling his shirt up to reveal a T-shirt with the number '100' scrawled on it in black felt-pen. "I'd been waiting to do that for two or three games," he recalls. "By the time I scored the felt pen had worn out a bit."

As Steve McManaman said after the match: "He deserved to break Rush's record because he has been absolutely magnificent. He has plenty of composure in the box [and] his awareness is incredible."

On Christmas Day 1996, Liverpool's 1—1 draw away to Newcastle had put them three points clear of Arsenal at the top of the Premiership table and everybody on Merseyside was beginning to say that this was Liverpool's year. Despite injury, Robbie had already clocked up 19 goals and the team were still involved in four different competitions.

But from here on in, Liverpool's season would slump alarmingly. Some blamed what they perceived as the team's tendency to make ten passes when one more direct boot of the ball would do the same job. Some blamed what

they saw as Liverpool's lack of 'bottle', that gritty spirit that had seen the Liverpool teams of the Seventies and Eighties tough it out against the world's best and win.

Mostly though, you'd have to blame bad luck. There were several matches which Liverpool could — should — have won. The 0—0 draw at home to Blackburn, in which Robbie missed at least five sitters, for example. ("He doesn't usually miss that many in a whole season," said McAteer.) Or the surprise 2—1 defeat at home to lowly Coventry, who last won at Anfield when dinosaurs roamed the earth...

Liverpool enjoyed better luck in Europe, where Robbie scored one of the goals of the season during yet another comeback from injury in the hard-earned 1—1 draw in Norway to SK Brann, in the quarter-finals of the Cup Winners' Cup. Liverpool made the breakthrough after just ten minutes with a wonderful flowing move, started by Ruddock, who found Stig Bjornebye who headed the ball on to Robbie. With SK defender Erik Skjaelaaen breathing down his neck, Robbie cheekily flicked the ball over his head before firing the ball home for his 22nd goal of the season and arguably his best.

"That was a truly great strike from Robbie," Roy Evans agreed. Two more goals from Robbie at Anfield in the return leg, a crushing 3—0 victory, ensured Liverpool cruised into the semi-finals and took Robbie's European tally for the season to six goals in five matches.

Robbie had celebrated his second goal by pulling his shirt up over his head to reveal a new T-shirt message that read: 'Support Liverpool Dockers: Sacked since September'.

Robbie hits one on the turn to put Liverpool 1–0 up against Nottingham Forest at the City Ground...

It was a reference to the long-running industrial dispute at the city's dockyard that had resulted in 500 dockers being sacked. "Macca gave me the shirt and asked me to wear it and he had one on as well," Robbie explained afterwards. (McManaman's shirt with the same message was seen when he exchanged shirts with one of the Norwegians at the end of the game.)

Unfortunately, UEFA regulations prohibit players from displaying political logos at matches. (Norwegian players were censured in 1996 for unfurling a banner before a friendly international protesting at French nuclear tests in the South Pacific.) Robbie was sure to be reprimanded by FIFA. But the Liverpool dockers were understandably delighted. Jim Davies, spokesman for the Merseyside Port shop stewards, said: "It is fantastic. Robbie and Steve are both local lads and have been very supportive of our cause. Their actions at the game have given us massive exposure. It is a shot in the arm for all the dockers."

Robbie's scruples became the cause of even more controversy when Liverpool travelled to Highbury for their vital Premiership match, in March. With both teams neck-and-neck behind leaders Manchester United and everything to play for, a Mark Wright pass put Robbie through in the first half but as he ran the ball into the penalty area, Arsenal keeper David Seaman appeared to bring him down. Referee Gerald Ashby immediately blew for a penalty but — incredibly — Robbie ran over to speak to the clearly startled ref, insisting that Seaman had never touched him (as TV replays confirmed) and that it wasn't a penalty.

But his protests fell on deaf ears as Ashby pointed to the spot. Robbie took the kick himself, firing weakly to the left of Seaman, who saved the effort only to see Jason McAteer score from the rebound. The goal put Liverpool into a 2–0 lead, later reduced by an Ian Wright goal, but Liverpool hung on for the victory that lifted them to within three points of Manchester United.

"Our lads are still sick at the penalty decision but they all appreciate what Robbie tried to do," said Seaman. He brought smiles when asked what more Robbie could have done, he responded: "He could have kicked the penalty wide."

Defensive frailty: Fowler slips in to score again...

Professional Footballers' Association chief executive Gordon Taylor said: "It was an excellent example set by one of our younger players, who has on occasions been portrayed as a scallywag. You do see this kind of honesty occasionally but not enough. He said immediately it was not a penalty and that he didn't want David Seaman sent off. In my opinion, the very fact he said what he did kept David on the field."

The Times called it 'a moment of Corinthian spirit on the moneyed sportsfields of Great Britain' and Sepp Blatter, the President of FIFA, personally sent a fax to Robbie at Anfield, thanking him for his action.

Ironically, Robbie also got a fax that week from UEFA's Control and Disciplinary Committee, informing him that he had been fined £900 for his little show of support for the dockers. Shadow Sports Minister Tom Pendry condemned Fowler's punishment as 'excessive', and PFA chief executive Gordon Taylor criticised UEFA's 'high-handed attitude'.

Speaking for the first time about it, Robbie shrugged and said: "I never expected all this fuss. I did the same thing against Chelsea this season, when I went over their goalkeeper but the referee had given a goal kick. I just wanted to make it clear to the referee on Monday that David

Seaman hadn't touched me. I got up straight away and went to walk away. I really couldn't believe it when the ref gave a penalty." He added hopefully that the reaction to his behaviour might help him get rid of his scallywag public image. "I am described by a lot of people as a bit of a rogue, but maybe what I did might change a few minds."

The most headline-grabbing week of his career was rounded off when Glenn Hoddle selected Robbie for his second full appearance for England, in their friendly against Mexico, at Wembley on March 29. Sheringham had put England ahead from the penalty spot in the 18th minute after defender Pavel Pardo tripped Paul Ince in the box. And Robbie finally scored his first goal for England, sealing a 2–0 victory with a fine header from six feet out.

Once he got off the mark, all the assurance he displays for his club came to the surface. "He's been earmarked as a future international player and it's up to him to adjust to international football," Hoddle said. "We've seen Gary Lineker and Alan Shearer develop along those lines and Robbie has a lot of hard work ahead of him. But he has the talent to achieve their status."

The England goal was Robbie's 29th of the season. He said: "It's been a bit of a difficult week, but I felt under no real pressure and it was just nice to go out there and score a goal in an England win."

Unfortunately, it was to be a last hurrah as first Liverpool crashed 3–0 away to Paris St Germain in the first leg of the semi-finals of the Cup Winners' Cup. Then Robbie brought his own season to a premature close by getting sent off against Everton, after he and defender David Unsworth had a punch-up that started on the pitch and continued into the tunnel. It meant Robbie would be fined £1000 by the FA for 'misconduct' and, more crucially, was suspended for Liverpool's last three League games of the season.

Robbie's last game of the season was against Manchester United, at Anfield on April 19. With just four games left, Liverpool lay second in the Premiership, just two points behind United. Victory would put Liverpool top of the table, a point clear and the pressure would be back on United. But two almost identical headed goals from Gary Pallister and a final nod into the net from Andy Cole when James appeared to fumble a high cross were enough to cancel out Barnes's solitary retaliatory strike in the 19th minute. United were able to rub salt into the wound by romping home not just with the title-clinching three points but with their biggest League win at Anfield for 28 years.

From that point on, though, Liverpool's season was effectively over. Though they saved some pride by battering Paris St Germain 2–0 in the return leg at Anfield (Robbie got the first after just 12 minutes — his 13th in Cup competitions overall and his 31st of the season), the Cup Winners' Cup would remain a dream for another year. As would the

ROBBIE FOWLER: FACTS, STATS AND STAR-SPEAK!

IAN WRIGHT (ARSENAL AND ENGLAND)

"Robbie can be around for England for the next ten years. It's up to him and how he approaches it. But he wants to achieve and do well, and he's doing it the right way. I know you can work really hard and just not get the breaks in the box. But Robbie got one chance [against Mexico] and took it... He's a fantastic forward and I just want him to go on and represent us at world level."

Capped for his country...

STEVE McMANAMAN (LIVERPOOL AND ENGLAND)

"I can't see any reason why [Robbie] and Alan Shearer should not form a partnership. They are very different types of players and they have attributes that can complement each other. On top of that, they are both goalscorers at the very top level — and that surely has to be a delicious prospect for England."

GRAEME SOUNESS (FORMER LIVERPOOL MANAGER)

"Robbie Fowler is someone who, without exaggeration, could go on and be even better than some of the greatest strikers Liverpool have had in recent history. He's got everything. He can finish with either foot. he's strong, he's brave... He's got everything to be the very best."

IAN RUSH (LEEDS UNITED)

"I've got a lot of records out of Liverpool, but I think if he's at Liverpool for the next five or ten years, I'll be very surprised if I have any records left. Because if there's one person that's going to break them, it'll be Robbie."

GLENN HODDLE (ENGLAND COACH)

"He's a born scorer. We've seen Alan Shearer and Gary Lineker develop and I think Robbie's another one who could go that way. He's got a lot of hard work ahead of him but he can achieve that by the time he's 26 or 27, that's when he will be in his prime."

JOHN BARNES (LIVERPOOL)

"If you are looking for goalscorers, Robbie has to be up there with the best of them. He has the temperament, self-belief, arrogance, whatever you want to call it... He has probably missed more chances than he has ever scored. But that's not going to be a problem for Robbie Fowler — we just have to create the chances for Robbie to put them away."

GOAL PROWLER: ROBBIE'S COMPLETE LEAGUE RECORD

Season	Games	Goals
1991—2	-	-
1992—3	-	-
1993—4	28	12
1994—5	42	25
1995—6	38	28
1996—7	33	18
Total:	141	83

STEVIE MAC: THE LOWDOWN ON ROBBIE'S BEST PAL

Born in Kirby, Stevie Mac is three years older than his best mate and has already become world famous as one of the stars of England's so-nearly-successful Euro 96 team. An attacking midfielder who prefers a free role just behind the strikers, Steve has not and will never score as many goals as Robbie, but it is his penetrating runs and passes that have provided Robbie, Rush, Collymore and Berger with some of the best of their goals for Liverpool over the last three years.

A possible future Liverpool captain, he is also seen as a good influence on the youngsters at Anfield (he has his own weekly column in *The Times*) and as a sensible and intelligent friend for Robbie to rely on as he reaches for the top of the footballing tree.

In action for
England

Coca-Cola Cup joy
for Robbie and
Jamie Redknapp

Premiership, as United strolled home with a paltry 75 points, while Newcastle, Arsenal and Liverpool all fell in behind them with 68 each. They even missed out on a chance of qualifying for the European Champions League next time round when Newcastle pipped them to second place with a slightly better goal difference.

It had been a disappointing end to a season that had promised so much. But Robbie, as ever, refuses to be down-beat about it. Instead, he is already looking forward to next season, as he fights to win Liverpool that elusive Premiership title and hopes to continue impressing Glenn Hoddle enough to take him with him to the World Cup in France next summer.

Still plagued by injuries, he missed England's World Cup qualifier against Poland in May as well as the outstanding Le Tournoi performances that followed it. He was having surgery on his adenoids. "I have had the problem for years. It is why I wear a nose band but it is getting worse. I want to get it sorted out as soon as possible."

But, says Glenn Hoddle, "The door will never be shut on anyone because going into a World Cup you need players who are full of confidence and are fit... It will be a great season with players trying to break into the squad."

Robbie knows that with Alan Shearer wearing the Number 9 shirt for England, he may have to wait a while for his chance. "You can't see anybody keeping him out. He's proved what a good striker he is. He's England's number one and rightly so. But there is always the hope of being paired with him if I keep doing well in club football, and that's got to be my long-term aim. The sooner I get a few more starts for England the better, even though I'm young yet."

The new season will see several new faces in the Anfield dressing room. The £3.7 million arrival of Oyvind Leonhardsen from Wimbledon was swiftly followed by the signing for £4.2 million of Inter Milan and England mid-field-general Paul Ince, and Evans also snapped up Crewe's England Under-20 starlet Danny Murphy for £1.5 million. New reserve keepe, Jorgen Nielsen has also been recruited to keep David James on his toes.

With Stan the Man gone for £7 million to Aston Villa, Evans made a daring swoop for Karl-Heinz Riedle of Borussia Dortmund, signing the 31-year-old hitman for £1.3 million. The raid took Evans's total spend in perparation for the new season up to an impressive £12 million and ensured Liverpool will be a force to be reckoned with.

cameras at England
training and
dreaming of glory

Not that it really matters who Robbie has behind him. As Jamie Redknapp says with only a slight hint of humour: "Robbie could play up front with his mum and still score goals."

Robbie himself has pledged his long-term future to Liverpool and says he wants to spend the rest of his career with Liverpool chasing the scoring records of Anfield legends Ian Rush and Roger Hunt.

"I'm well off at Liverpool and I'm not interested in moving abroad. A lot of foreign players are coming over here now, which proves we are going the right way and I don't see any reason why I should want to play in another league when this will be one of the best in the world.

"The atmosphere in the grounds is first class, you play against good teams, and players. The likes of the Vialli's —

how many European trophies as he won? To play against these guys is incentive enough to stay at Liverpool in itself."

Besides, according to Robbie, Liverpool are going to win the League this year. "We've already got a lot of good players at Liverpool and I reckon we're a better team than Man United. We've played United plenty of times in recent seasons and won more games than we've lost.

"We've had criticism from the press who say that we're not hungry enough to win the Premier League. That's nonsense.

"We have been growing up together over the last couple of seasons and now we have the self-belief to win the title. We have improved over that period and now I am very confident we will have a trophy to show for our efforts next season, even though there is still a lot of work to do."

And goals to score...